MINIBEASTS UP CLOSE

Mosquitoes Up Close

Robin Birch

Chicago, Illinois

Published by Raintree, a division of Reed Elsevier, Inc.
Chicago, Illinois
Customer Service 888-363-4266
Visit our website at www.raintreelibrary.com

For information, address the publisher:
Raintree, 100 N. LaSalle, Suite 1200, Chicago, IL 60602

09 08 07 06 05
10 9 8 7 6 5 4 3 2 1

Printed and bound in Hong Kong and China by WKT Company Limited.

Library of Congress Cataloging-in-Publication Data

Birch, Robin.
Mosquitoes up close / Robin Birch.
p. cm. -- (Minibeasts up close)
Includes bibliographical references (p. 30).
ISBN 1-4109-1141-1 -- ISBN 1-4109-1148-9
1. Mosquitoes--Juvenile literature. I. Title. II. Series: Birch, Robin. Minibeasts up close.
QL536.B565 2004
595.77'2--dc22

2004003112

Acknowledgments
The publisher would like to thank the following for permission to reproduce photographs:
pp. 4, 16, 19 © Paul Zborowski; p. 5 David M. Dennis/Auscape/OSF; p. 6 Corbis; p. 7 Bruce Cowell/© Queensland Museum; p. 8 Science Photo Library/Dr Pete Billingsley, University of Aberdeen/Sinclair Stammers; p. 10 Eye of Science/Science Photo Library; p. 11 Martin Dohrn/Nature Picture Library; p. 13 David Scharf/Science Photo Library; p. 14 Dr Tony Brain/Science Photo Library; p. 15 © Holt Studios/DWSPL; pp. 17, 24 © Jiri Lochman/Lochman Transparencies; p. 18 Peter Parks/NHPA Limited; pp. 22-23 Alan Blank/Bruce Coleman Inc; p. 26 Sinclair Stammers/Science Photo Library; p. 27 Martin Dohrn/Science Photo Library; p. 28 Hampton (RM)/DWSPL; p. 29 Dale Mann.

Cover photograph of mosquito reproduced with permission of Noah Poritz/photolibrary.com/SPL.

Every effort has been made to contact copyright holders of any material reproduced in this book. Any omissions will be rectified in subsequent printings if notice is given to the publisher.

Contents

Any words appearing in bold, **like this,** are explained in the Glossary.

Amazing Mosquitoes!

Have you been bitten by a mosquito? Have you heard the buzzing noise a mosquito makes? Have you wondered what mosquitoes are really like?

Mosquitoes are amazing when you get to know them close up. They have mouths with tiny needles in them for feeding on animals and plants. If a mosquito bites you, it is a female. Male mosquitoes only feed on plants.

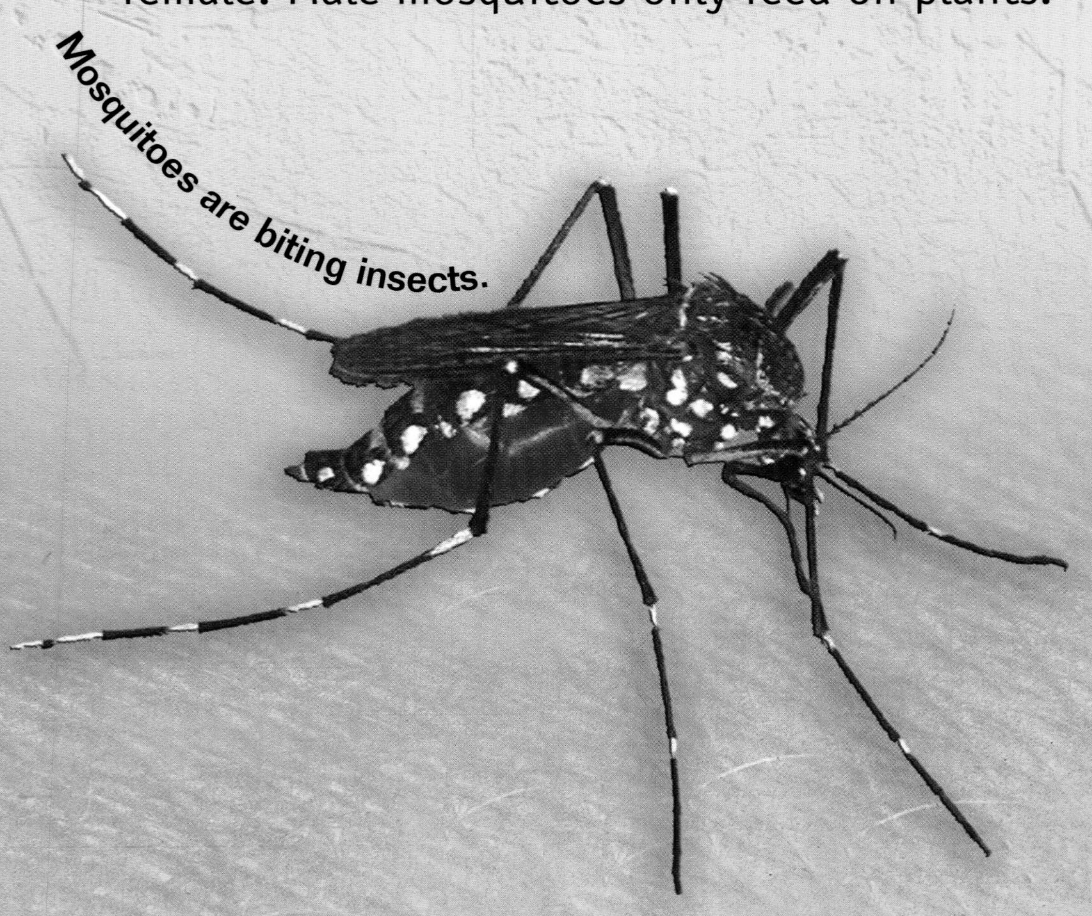

Mosquitoes are biting insects.

What are mosquitoes?

A mosquito is a type of fly. The word *mosquito* means "little fly" in Spanish.

A mosquito is an insect. Insects are animals that have six legs. They also have a hard skin on the outside of the body called an **exoskeleton,** instead of bones on the inside.

How many?

There are more than 2,500 kinds, or **species,** of mosquitoes in the world. The smallest is the size of the head of a pin, and the largest is about as long as one of your fingers.

Where Do Mosquitoes Live?

Mosquitoes are found in most parts of the world. They are very small and dry out easily. Because of this, most of them prefer moist, calm air.

Mosquitoes usually rest in dark places, away from bright light. They rest on tree trunks and among grasses. They also rest inside bushes and trees, in rock holes, animal holes, and caves. Others live inside buildings.

This pond of calm, fresh water has plenty of places for mosquitoes to live.

Living near water

Most mosquitoes lay their eggs on the surface of calm, fresh water. The water may be in tin cans, barrels, pools, puddles, ditches, or marshes. The mosquitoes find water sheltered from the wind by grass or weeds.

Most female mosquitoes cannot fly very far. They live near water so they do not have to fly far to lay their eggs. The males also live near water because they follow the females.

Hiding

Some mosquitoes are colored or patterned so they can hide on a tree trunk or on a flower. This is called camouflage.

Mosquito Body Parts

A mosquito has a long, thin body. The body is in three parts. First is the head, then the **thorax** in the middle, and then the **abdomen** at the end.

The head

The head has large eyes, long feelers called **antennae,** and mouthparts. The mouthparts are **palps** and a long, thin **proboscis.**

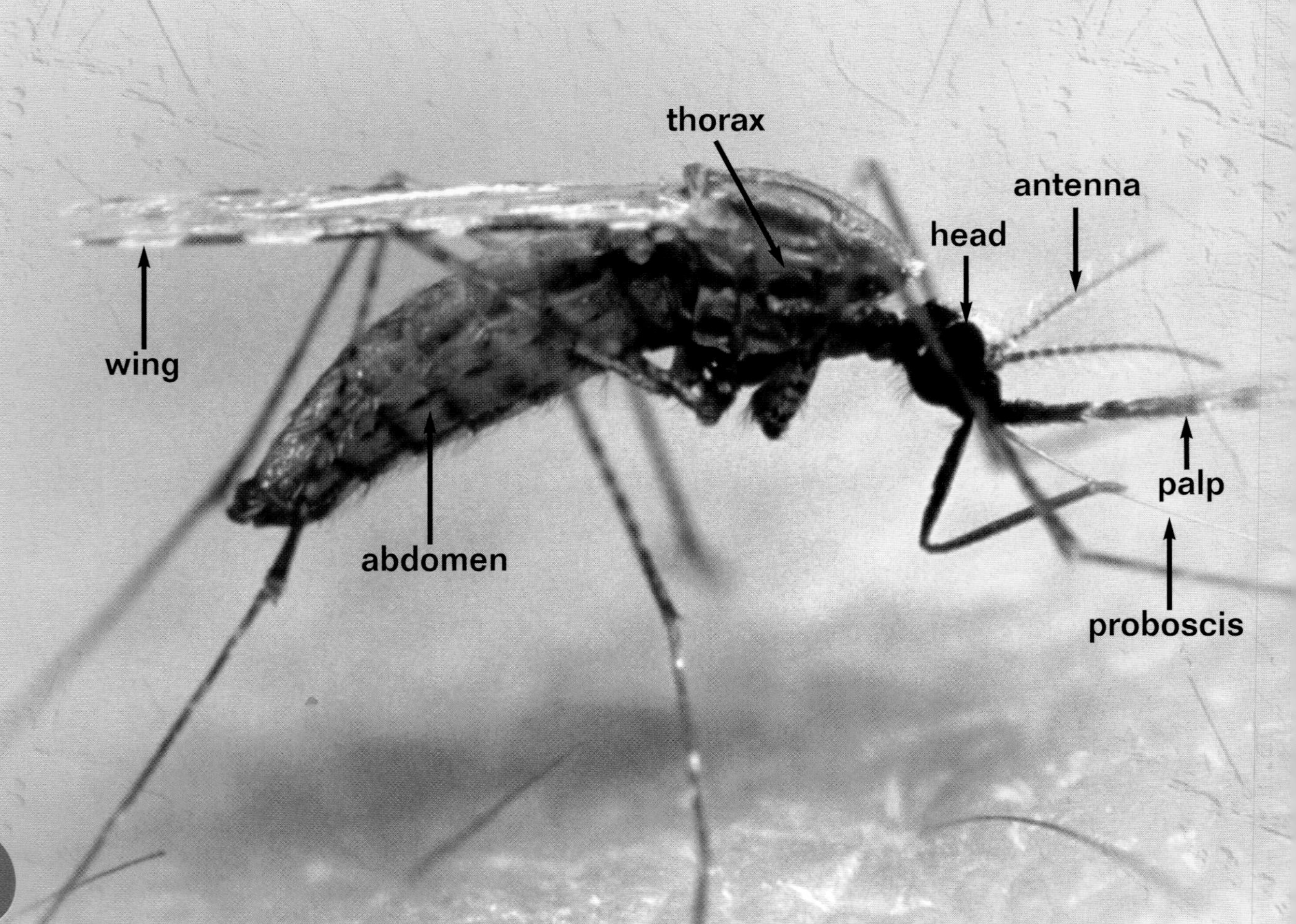

The thorax

The thorax has six legs and two wings joined to it.

Head down

Anopheles mosquitoes stand with their heads down low and abdomen up high. They hold their back legs high up in the air.

The abdomen

The abdomen is long and thin. It has either two claws or two flaps on the end.

The exoskeleton

A mosquito's **exoskeleton** covers its whole body. It gives the mosquito its shape and protects it from being hurt easily. It also keeps the mosquito from drying out by trapping water inside its body.

The exoskeleton has hairs on it. The mosquito uses these hairs to feel or touch things. The exoskeleton has tiny **spines** as well.

Mouthparts and Eating

Both male and female mosquitoes feed on plant juices such as **nectar** and sap. Most female mosquitoes also drink blood. They bite animals such as **mammals,** birds, snakes, frogs, and insects.

Mosquitoes have a **palp**, like a finger, on each side of the **proboscis**. A mosquito feels and tastes food with its palps.

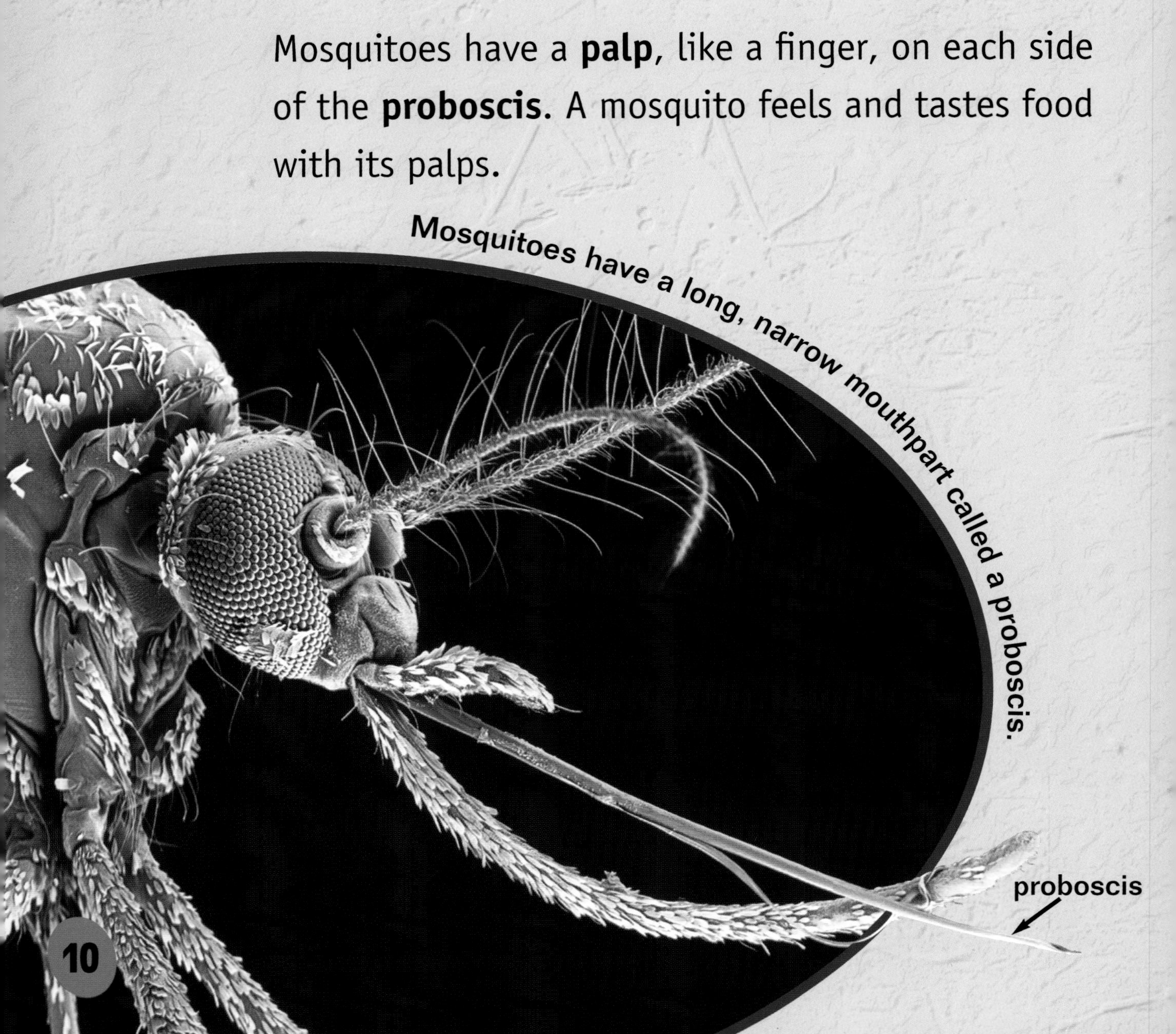

Mosquitoes have a long, narrow mouthpart called a proboscis.

How mosquitoes bite

Female mosquitoes that bite animals have six long, thin needles inside the proboscis. When a mosquito bites, it cuts the skin with the sharp needles and pokes them in.

The female mosquito sucks up blood through one of the needles. While this is happening, **saliva** flows down another needle into the skin. The saliva keeps the blood runny, so the mosquito can drink it. The mosquito's saliva makes the animal's skin swollen and itchy.

The female mosquito's abdomen fills with blood as she drinks blood through the proboscis.

Eyes and Seeing

A mosquito has a large eye on each side of its head. Its eyes cover most of the sides and front of its head. A mosquito can see all around it with its large eyes.

Each eye is made up of hundreds of very small eyes. This kind of eye is called a **compound** eye. The small eyes each have six sides and are packed closely together. Each small eye faces in a slightly different direction, and sees something a little bit different from the other small eyes.

Swarms

Sometimes, mosquitoes hover in a large group called a swarm. They watch the other mosquitoes in the swarm so they can keep their place in the group.

What do mosquitoes see?

Mosquitoes use their eyes to find food. They seem to prefer biting dark-colored things. For example, they bite people with dark-colored clothes rather than bright or light clothes.

This close-up photograph shows how each compound eye is made up of many small eyes.

Antennae and Sensing

Mosquitoes have two long feelers called **antennae.** The antennae are on the head, between the eyes.

Hairy antennae

The antennae are made of many small sections. Each section has a circle of hairs around the end. On female mosquitoes, the hairs are short and there are not many of them. On male mosquitoes, there are many long hairs.

Male mosquitoes have bushy antennae.

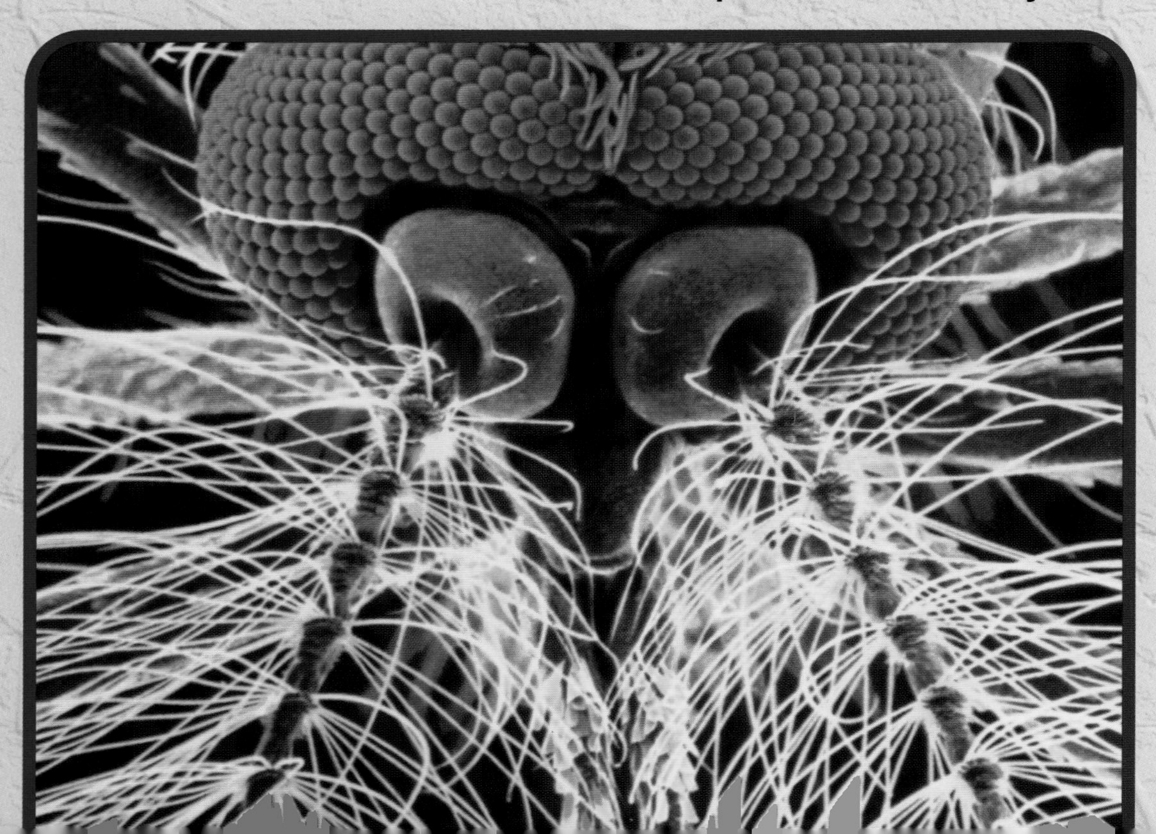

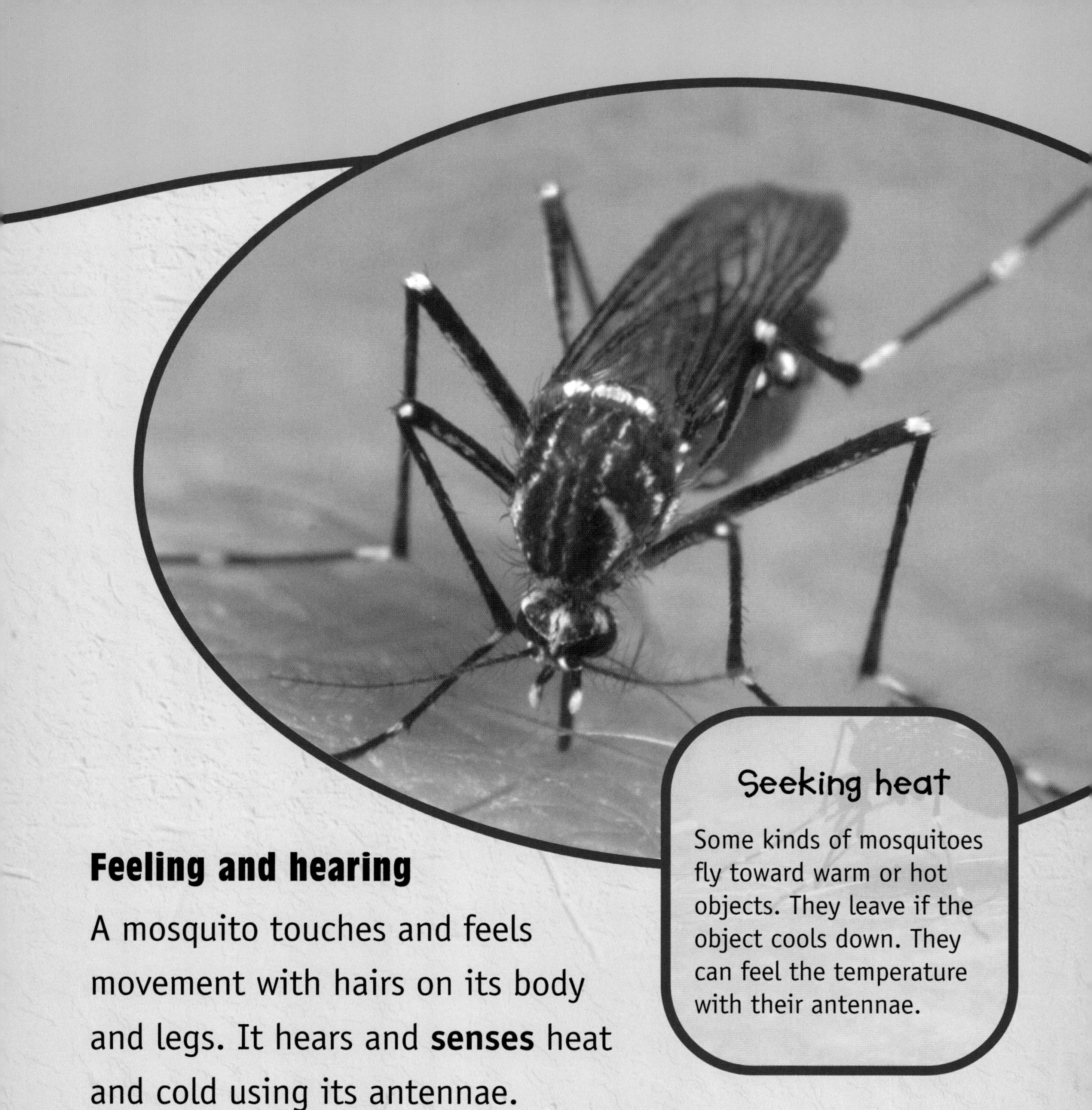

Seeking heat

Some kinds of mosquitoes fly toward warm or hot objects. They leave if the object cools down. They can feel the temperature with their antennae.

Feeling and hearing

A mosquito touches and feels movement with hairs on its body and legs. It hears and **senses** heat and cold using its antennae.

Smelling and tasting

A mosquito smells with its antennae. It tastes with its mouthparts and with hairs on its feet.

Legs for Moving

A mosquito has six legs, three on each side of its **thorax.** Each leg has three main parts, and a long foot.

Mosquitoes are flying insects. They walk only very short distances. They use their legs and feet to hold on to animals and plants while they are feeding. A mosquito also uses its legs to stand while resting, and while it lays its eggs.

Mosquitoes have long, thin legs attached to the thorax.

Legs as antennae

A mosquito feels movements in the air with its legs. When a mosquito is biting or resting, it holds its back legs high in the air. It uses them as extra **antennae.** They help the mosquito **sense** danger.

Mosquitoes hold their back legs up in the air when they bite. This mosquito is biting a frog.

Which way up?

If a mosquito lands on a wall, it always faces up. Its front and middle legs sense whether the mosquito is facing up or down.

Running on water

Some of the *Sabethes* mosquitoes have a wide paddle on each leg made of long hairs. The paddles may help them run on the surface of water.

Wings and Flying

A mosquito flies to find food, places to lay eggs, and resting places.

A mosquito has two wings. The shape of the wings is made by veins, which are hard, empty tubes. The wings have **scales** on them. The scales lie along the veins and look like fringes on the back edges of the wings.

Most insects have two pairs of wings, but mosquitoes have only one pair.

Flying

Mosquitoes can fly forward, backward, straight up, or straight down. They can hover in one place and turn around in place. The wings beat very fast, which makes a buzzing sound.

Mosquitoes have small knobs, called halteres, on the **thorax** behind the wings. The halteres shake very fast when a mosquito flies. This helps the mosquito balance when it is flying.

This is a close-up photograph of a mosquito's wing.

The Thorax and Abdomen

A mosquito's **thorax** has six legs and two wings joined to it.

The **abdomen** has eight sections. The sections make stripes across the abdomen. The male has two claws on the end of his abdomen. The female has two small flaps on the end of her abdomen.

How do mosquitoes get air?

There are ten air holes called **spiracles** on each side of the body. Mosquitoes take in air through these holes. Tiny tubes carry air around the body.

The heart

The heart is long and thin, and runs down the middle of the abdomen. It pumps blood around the body.

What happens to food?

When the mosquito sucks blood, a pump in the mosquito's throat pushes the blood into the food stomach. There also is a storage stomach for storing the plant liquid that the mosquito drinks. This juice is let into the food stomach a little at a time.

When the food stomach is full, the abdomen swells up. The mosquito passes waste through its **anus.**

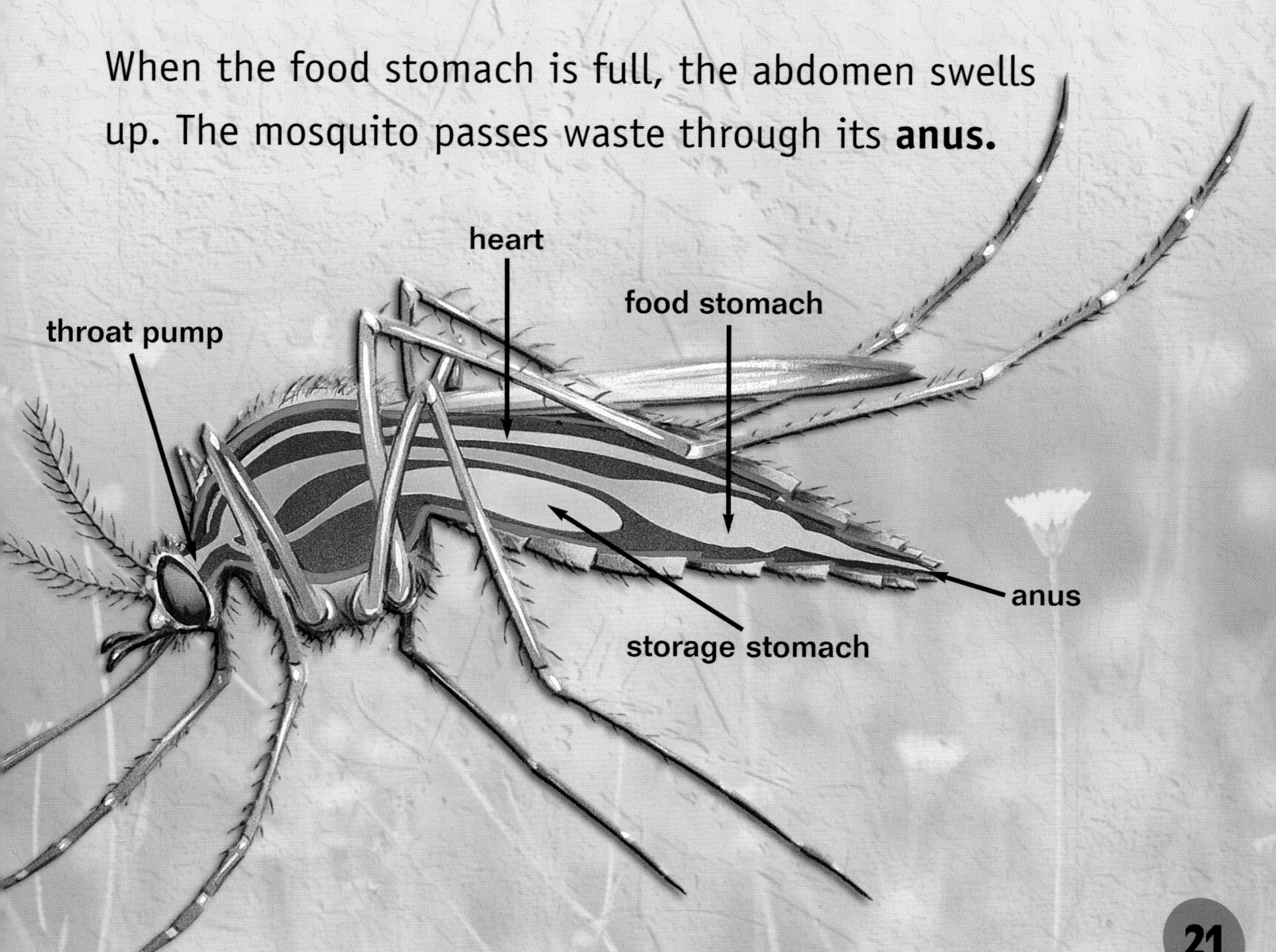

Mosquito Eggs

Mosquitoes grow from eggs. First the female mosquito **mates** with a male mosquito. Then she lays her eggs.

A female usually lays her eggs on water. Some mosquitoes lay their eggs on damp soil that will be flooded with water later.

Raft made of eggs

Often, many eggs are joined together to make a raft. An egg raft floats on the water. Some mosquitoes do not make rafts. They leave each egg by itself on the water.

Some kinds of mosquitoes make rafts of up to 400 eggs.

Hatching

Most eggs hatch within 48 hours. Other eggs wait during a cold winter before hatching. Eggs usually need water before they will hatch. This is because the young mosquito that hatches will die if it does not have water to live in.

Long egg rafts

Coquillettidia mosquitoes have egg rafts with a long, narrow shape, like a boat. These eggs are always laid on water that has plants growing up through it or floating on it.

Mosquito Larvae

A mosquito hatches out of its egg as a **larva.** The larva lives in the water. It has a head and a body with no legs. The larva is called a wriggler because it swims by wriggling, or wiggling. A mosquito is a wriggler for between four and fourteen days.

Wrigglers hang upside down from the water's surface and take in air through a breathing tube.

Breathing

Most wrigglers have a breathing tube on the back end of the body. The wriggler hangs from the surface of the water, breathing through the tube.

Big wrigglers

Toxorhynchites mosquitoes are the largest mosquitoes. They have huge wrigglers, which eat the wrigglers and pupae of other kinds of mosquitoes.

Eating

Wrigglers feed on **microorganisms** and rotting plants and animals in the water. They feed all the time because they are growing fast. They have **vibrating** brushes made of hair near their mouths. These help gather food drifting in the water.

Growing

As the wriggler grows, it gets too big for its skin. It splits its skin open and comes out so that it can keep growing. This is called molting. It molts four times,and then it becomes a **pupa.**

Becoming an Adult

While a mosquito is a **pupa,** it changes from a **larva** into an adult mosquito. The mosquito pupa is called a tumbler. This is because when it moves, it makes a jerking, tumbling movement in the water.

A tumbler does not eat. Most of the time it floats at the surface of the water and breathes through two tubes called trumpets.

Tumblers have two paddles on the end of their tails. They move by flipping their tails.

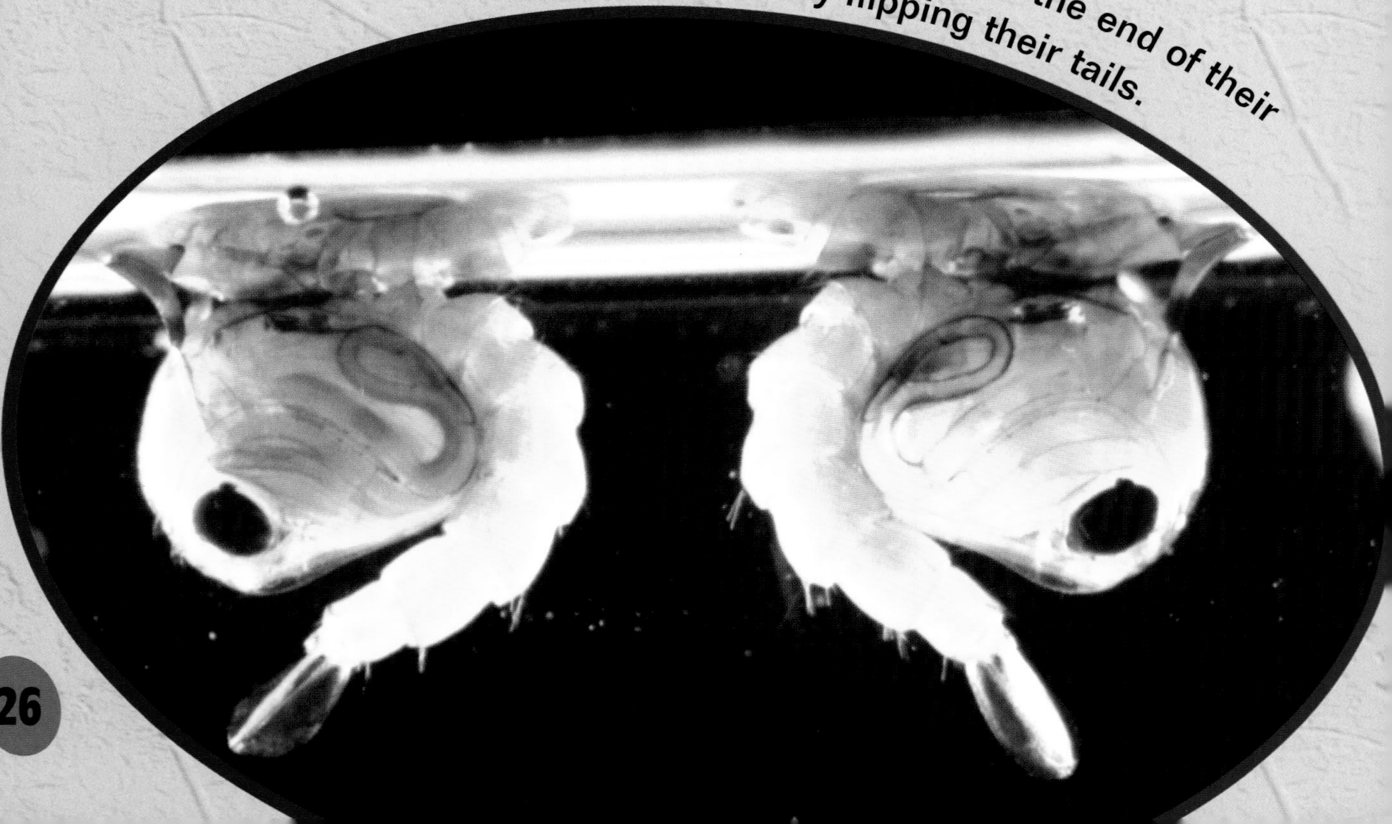

Adult mosquito

A mosquito is a pupa for a few days. The pupa's skin then splits open and the adult mosquito comes out.

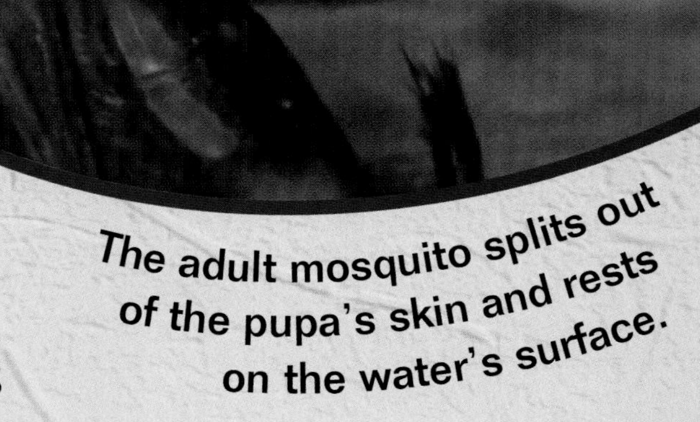

The adult mosquito splits out of the pupa's skin and rests on the water's surface.

After the mosquito has come out of the pupa's skin, it rests on the surface of the water for a short time. It dries out a little and its **exoskeleton** becomes hard. The wings spread out and dry so that the mosquito can fly.

Soon it has its first meal, which is usually some flower **nectar.**

Mosquitoes and Us

We are more likely to get bitten by mosquitoes when we are outside in the evening, after dark. This is when there are more mosquitoes about. There may be mosquitoes around if there is water nearby.

The itchy mark of a mosquito bite can last for a few days.

Diseases

Some mosquitoes spread diseases when they bite. One of the diseases mosquitoes give people in some hot, wet places is malaria.

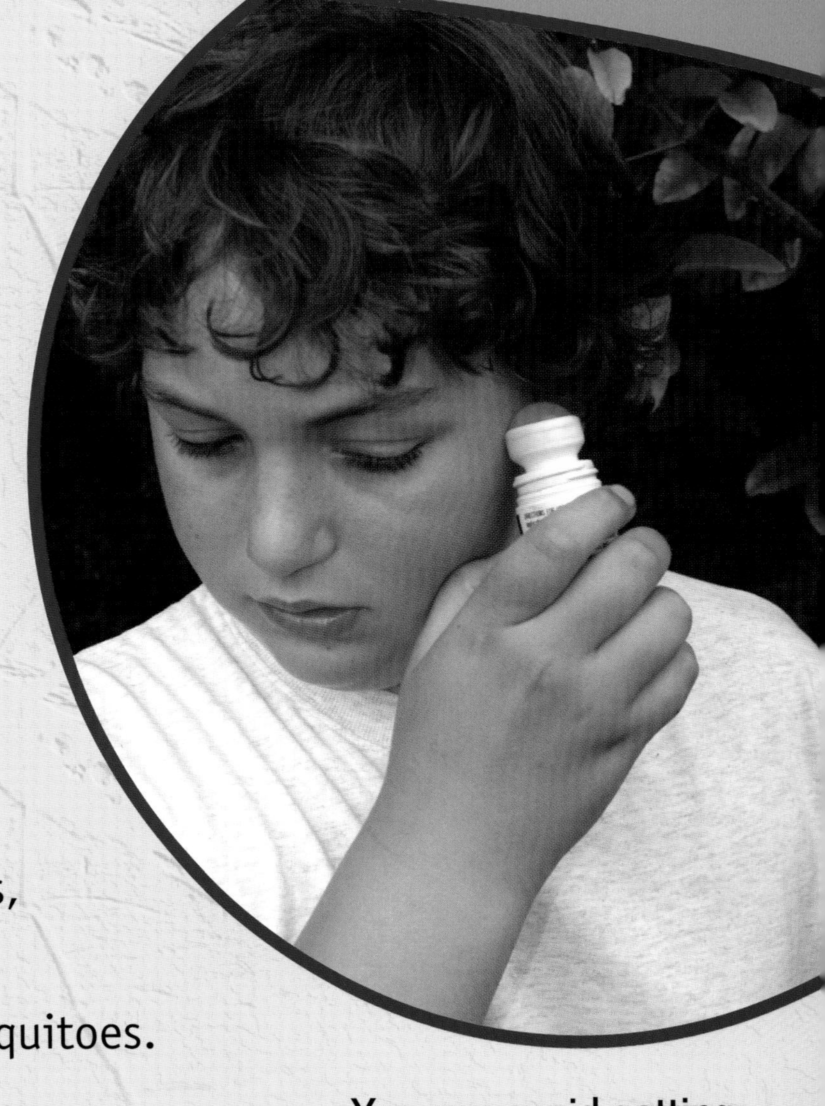

Mosquito predators

Many animals eat mosquitoes. Birds, bats, dragonflies, lizards, bugs, spiders, frogs, and toads are all **predators** of mosquitoes.

Mosquitoes may be annoying to people, but without them there would be less food for many animals.

You can avoid getting mosquito bites by using a repellant. Mosquitoes do not like its smell.

Find Out for Yourself

You may know where there is a pool of calm water. You could put some of the water in a jar and look at it closely. See if there are mosquito wrigglers or tumblers in it. Make sure you wash your hands after you collect the water. You could also watch the pool for mosquitoes above the surface. What are they doing?

Books to read

Claybourne, Anna. *Insects*. Chicago: Raintree, 2002.

McDonald, Mary Ann. *Mosquitoes*. Eden Prairie, Minn.: Child's World, 2000.

Meister, Cari. *Mosquitoes*. Edina, Minn.: ABDO Publishing, 2001.

Spilsbury, Louise and Richard Spilsbury. *The Life Cycle of Insects*. Chicago: Heinemann Library, 2003.

Using the Internet

Explore the Internet to find out more about mosquitoes. Have an adult help you use a search engine. Type in a keyword such as *mosquitoes* or the name of a particular mosquito.

Glossary

abdomen last of the three main sections of an insect

antenna (plural: antennae) feeler on an insect's head

anus hole in the abdomen through which droppings pass

compound made up of smaller parts

exoskeleton hard outside skin of an insect

larva (plural: larvae) young stage of many insects, a grub

mammal animal that has hair, is warm-blooded and feeds its young milk

mate when a male and a female come together to produce young

microorganism tiny living thing, so small it can only be seen with a microscope

nectar sweet juice in flowers

palp small body part like a finger, near an insect's mouth

predator animal that kills and eats another animal

proboscis long, thin mouthpart

pupa (plural: pupae) stage of an insect's life, when it changes from a larva to an adult

repellent something that keeps things away from it

saliva liquid from the mouth

scale small, hard, flat object

sense how an animal knows what is going on around it, such as by hearing, seeing, or smelling

species type or kind of animal; animals of the same species can produce young together

spine hard, pointed spike

spiracle tiny air hole on an insect's body

thorax chest part of an insect

vibrating shaking quickly

Index